Seed of the Woman

By

Pastor Sarah Morgan

ACKNOWLEDGEMENTS

To the staff at CSN, thank you for working hard to meet the deadline.

To all my daughters in Zion, especially Shirley Brown, Dawn Gray and Annie Umoh, who never gave up on me. Thank you for pushing me into destiny.

To the Vision family – your prayers and financial support enabled me to fulfill this dream.

To Brandon Brown – good job with the tape ministry. I told you it would all pay off one day.

And to my wonderful family, the Morgan's: Quincy, Joel, Jesse, Andrew, William, Joshua and Deborah. What would I do without you? Life is worth living because of you guys. I love you all.

Last, but not least, to my heavenly Father – the covenant-making and covenant-keeping God, to His Son Jesus, and my friend and partner, the Holy Spirit, without whom I am nothing and I can do nothing.

Thank you,
Pastor Sarah Morgan

DEDICATION

To the one who has selflessly poured into me the words of life. To the one whose words awakened the sleeping dreams, visions and aspirations that lay within me. To the one who taught me how to be bold, confident and courageous, to fear no one but to respect all men. To the one who assured me that "I could do all things through Christ who strengtheneth me." To the one who challenged me and provoked me to greatness. To the one who believed in me when I didn't believe in myself.

To this one I dedicate my first book. This one is my beloved and my friend. This one is my husband and my pastor, the honorable Bishop W. Peter Morgan.

Thank you for everything, for birthing the seed in me. I love you.

You wife,
Sarah Morgan

TABLE OF CONTENTS

CHAPTER ONE

Declaration of War

And the Lord God said to the woman, "What is this you have done?"

The woman said, "The serpent deceived me, and I ate."

So the Lord God said to the serpent:

Because you have done this, you are cursed more than all cattle, and more than every beast of the field; on your belly you shall go, and you shall eat dust all the days of your life. And I (God, Elohim, Yahweh, Jehovah) *will put enmity between you and the woman, and between your seed and her Seed; He* (some translations say 'it,' but the New King James says 'He,' because the Seed is a person; uppercase 'H,' so it's just not any person) *shall bruise your head, and you shall bruise His heel.*

(Genesis 3:13-15)

THIS MEANS WAR

You are licensed to bruise. The Word says the Seed will bruise and tread Satan's head underfoot. God Himself: Jehovah, the incorruptible God, Elohim, the Self-Existent One, He who has no beginning and no end, who is the beginning and the end, Yahweh, Adonai, the omnipotent, omnipresent, omniscient; the ubiquitous God Himself declared war on Satan. God looked the devil in the face and said, "It's on, Devil! You want it, it's on. I declare war between your seed and My seed; let the best man win!"

God declared war between the kingdom of the devil among men and His Kingdom. A war was proclaimed between the Seed of the woman and the seed of the serpent. War was proclaimed between good and evil, and between darkness and light.

"I WILL PUT ENMITY"

Since Creation, there has been enmity between man and the devil, just as God declared. Yes, there is a war going on, but the devil is in trouble! God wants us to know that the devil has had us for far too long. Our prophecy... is what we need to bruise the head of that power, that spirit, that demon that has tormented us, our families, our children, our businesses... God says, "That Seed is in your belly." This is a mystery that is about to be unveiled to the Body of Christ, (Col. 1:27).

IT IS IN YOU

You do not always have to run around looking for help from another prophecy, another man of God, another woman of God; because God wants you to know that you are already carrying the power, the Seed that you need to bruise Satan's head.

The devil, however, does not want you to come to church, to get up and pray, to get into the Word, because he knows that every time you are at church, praying, and reading the Word, you are activating the Seed that was prophesied by God Himself. And He said, "No matter how long it takes, Devil, you are on My calendar. The Seed of the woman: the same woman that you beguiled, the same woman that you deceived – the Seed out of the womb of that same woman will defeat you."

THE "KILLER" SEED

So the Seed of the woman shall bruise the head of the serpent: that demon, that power, that principality that has tormented you and stopped your progress. The Hebrew word is "zerà," meaning the Seed, the posterity of the woman, the offspring of the woman – the zerà shall bruise and destroy the head - not the tail, but the head.

What God is saying in Genesis 3:15 is that the Seed that is inside of you has been designed to bruise and to destroy the head of the serpent. You are licensed to bruise through the Word.

THE WORD WILL BE FULFILLED

When God declared war, in Gen. 3:15, the prophetic was released. What is the prophetic? "The prophetic" simply means "advance knowledge." When you have advance knowledge of something that is going to happen in the future, it is the prophetic; and to be forewarned means to be forearmed.

So God released the prophetic Word in the hearing of the devil, "For beguiling and deceiving the crown of My creation, I proclaim a war. The Seed of the woman will bruise your seed." And the Bible explains that when the prophetic was released, God set in motion the bringing forth of this prophecy. Over the thousands of years in Church history, this prophetic Word has been traveling from eternity to be fulfilled in time.

The only thing the devil fears more than anything is the prophetic Word that has been spoken over your life.

As long as you don't have a prophetic promise, the devil will not bother you. But the moment the prophetic is released upon your life, look out! He will fight you tooth and nail, because the war started not yesterday, not last year, not in the year 2000; the war started way back in the Garden of Eden, and the devil knows that God is God enough, that when He speaks, it must come to pass.

STAY UNDER COVER!

Satan was an anointed cherub who walked upon the fiery stones before the throne of God. He was not only an anointed cherub, but he was a "covering angel" who covered the throne of God. Because the devil was a covering angel, he knows the power and the significance of the covering, and so he will consistently try to get you out from under God's cover, (Eze. 28:14).

It is so important that you stay under the cover of the Lord! Satan knows that once you are under the covering, dwelling in the secret place of the Most High, abiding under the shadow of the Almighty, "A thousand may fall at your side, and ten thousand at your right hand; but it shall not come near you" (Psalm 91:7).

The gifts of the calling are without repentance. Satan knows his craft, he knows his gift. When he was kicked out of Heaven, his gift remained.

Satan's "Secret Files"

The same principle holds true in the case of personal assistants. Anyone who has been working closely with a director or manager has access to information that the rest of the company does not; access to "secret files."

That is why when companies fire personal assistants, there can be trouble, and they often have to pay the assistant a lot of money. So they think twice before they fire anyone... those they do not fire may be slienced! Why? Because they know too much and can endanger the company; they know things the company does not want released, and the company is vulnerable because of that secret information.

Similarly, when the devil and his cohorts were kicked out of Heaven, they came out with a certain degree of information. As a matter of fact, those fallen angels are what you hear when you seek information from palm readers, tarot card dealers or psychics. When that voice at the other end of the 1-800 number so accurately describes your "beau" and his car…that is a fallen spirit you are speaking to, using information Satan was privy to in Heaven.

WAGE A GOOD WARFARE

But remember, the devil is a liar! The only information he has is from your past; he has no information about your future. He is not omniscient and he is not omnipresent, so he only has information about your past. Therefore, he looms around in the background trying to hear God's plan for you. But nobody can frustrate that plan, abort it or miscarry it.

The Bible says,

> *This charge and admonition I commit in trust to you, Timothy, my son, in accordance with prophetic intimations which I formerly received concerning you, so that inspired and aided by them you may wage the good warfare.*
> (1 Timothy 1:18, AMP)

Paul told Timothy, "The devil, Timothy, is going to come after you. You are a young bishop, you are anointed, you are powerful. God has purpose and destiny for you, Timothy, and so the devil has targeted you. However, Timothy, I admonish you, I charge you that you wage

14

a good warfare against the devil, not with your works, not with a gun, not with a knife, but wage a good warfare with the prophecy."

So we are to wage a good warfare with the prophetic word that has been spoken, released, and dispersed into our spirits. Once that word has been released in eternity, it cannot return empty, it must accomplish the purpose for which it was sent, (Isa. 55:11).

It may be delayed, but it will be accomplished.

It may be held back but it will be accomplished.

It may be frustrated, but it will be accomplished.

LET THE PROPHECY LEAD

Many of us have died before our time; we have given up, dropped out of the race because we did not have the revelation. When you are a prophetic child carrying a prophetic Seed, no weapon that is formed, fashioned or sanctioned against you shall prosper. God's Word is clear on that point, (Isa. 54:17).

No matter how far down the devil pushes you, the prophetic word in you will always rise up. Even if you find yourself in the lion's den with lions all around, all of a sudden you will remember God's promise that you shall not die, but shall live and apply the works of Almighty God, (Pslm. 118:17)!

We have also a more sure word of prophecy; whereunto ye do well that ye take heed (pay close attention to it), as unto a light that shineth in a dark (dismal) place, until the day dawns (through the gloom), and the day star arise in your hearts (2 Peter 1:19, KJV) knowing this first, that no prophecy of Scripture is of any private interpretation, for prophecy never came by the will of man, but holy men of God spoke as they were moved by the Holy Spirit (2 Peter 1:20-21).

In other words, as long as you have a prophecy in your belly, there will be times and seasons of darkness: you may be unable to find your way and not know if you would rather live or die, but that prophetic word that is in your belly will serve as a light. It will guide you, it will lead you, and it will instruct you, because it's incorruptable.

In the midst of your dilemma it is dismal, it is dark and you cannot see the way, but God is saying there is a prophecy in your belly. So pull out your prophecy, let the porch light of the prophetic word begin to lead you in the path that you ought to follow, and before you know it, you will be out of the dark, (Prov. 4:18).

DWELL ON YOUR DESTINY

Joseph could have died. He could have gone to the bar and gotten drunk like some of us do when our future is bleak. But even when Potipher's wife was acting a fool, even in prison, Joseph remembered the prophecy, the prophetic dream in Gen. 37:5-9.. Every now and again he pulled it up and said, "God, this is not where you want me to be. This is not my destiny. This is not my purpose, God!"

"Where there is no vision the people perish" (Proverbs 29:18, KJV), because revelation drives us, revelation motivates us, revelation is what makes us walk differently despite those who are speaking maliciously about us. We are still able to stand tall because there is a revelation in our belly.

Job's friends saw him on his sick bed – he had lost weight, he had boils all over his body, his hair had fallen out - and they said, "I don't know if you're going to make it."

But because Job was a man who had a prophetic word in his belly, he said,

> *Though He slay me, yet will I trust Him. But He knows the way that I take; when He has tested me, I shall come forth as gold.*
> (Job 13:15; 23:10)

Job was speaking prophetically. In other words, "I will see it in my flesh, not in my grave. I have received a revelation from God that everything that I am going through is only a test, and when I come out of this I am going to receive double!"

Even in the Valleys

The Church, the Body of Christ, is intended to walk in the knowledge of this, to take heed to the prophetic word. God's Word is prophetic; we must allow that prophetic word in our bellies to be an under gird, to be a light, to be a torch when we are going through the valleys of life: the

17

valley of the shadow of death, the valley of Bakah or weeping, the valley of Jehoshaphat or decision, the valleys of poverty, lack and insufficiency. In those times the prophetic word in your belly should serve as a light, a "luminary" to illuminate your way, even if it is only a little at a time.

"Thy Word is a lamp unto my feet" (Psalm 119:105a, KJV). With merely a lamp lighting your way, how many steps can you safely take at a time? One step at a time! When you begin to step out in faith, it becomes *"a light unto your path"* (Psalm 119:105b, KJV); the light is thrown into your path. It is dark on the left and on the right, but there is a light which is illuminating out of your belly. Because of the prophetic word that God has deposited in you and because your lamp is lit, no matter how dark your situation, no matter how dark your circumstance, no matter how gloomy it looks or feels, you can find the way.

CHAPTER TWO

Dealing With the Devil

WATCHS OVER THE WORD
JER. 1:12, KJV

So we understand that our prophecy will light the way, no matter how dismal our circumstances. Sadly, the devil has also gotten a hold of this truth. Day and night Satan is watching over what the Body of Christ, the saints, are supposed to be watching over – the prophetic word in their bellies. The devil is watching over that prophetic word, and he is doing everything possible to frustrate it, to quench it, to crush it, to kill it, to abort it, to cause it to miscarry.

One morning you wake up and start acting all crazy. You are frustrated; you just lost your job, so you are angry. So you are going to drink yourself into oblivion, you are going to act crazy, you are going to act a fool – who do you think orchestrates that? Satan! He wants that prophetic word within you to be aborted.

The devil watches over your prophecy more than you do, over that word God has spoken into your life. God promises you are going to be great, mighty, powerful, and you know the deposit has been made, but you wake up in the morning and you start behaving like you are mediocre, like you are just a nobody. But when you are walking in cognizance and recognition of who you are and the prophetic word that is in you, you might be riding a bus, but you are a queen!

FOCUS ON THE FUTURE

I may be living in the projects right now, but I envision a house in Beverly Hills, because I see something in my belly. It is called the prophetic.

The knowledge of what you see in the realm of the Spirit determines how you walk as a child of God.

You may have only one suit, but when you walk in, everyone knows that you have arrived because the clothing, the Shekinah, the presence of God is all around you. There is just something about you, a confidence, because the revelation is in your belly.

A HISTORY OF EVIL

The devil also takes heed to the prophetic word, because he knows that when God speaks, it is established. So he will always seek to abort, to miscarry and to utterly destroy the seed before it becomes a tree.

When Eve conceived and gave birth to Cain and Abel, the devil remembered the prophetic word about the Seed of the woman. He immediately thought, "This must be it, because God said the Seed of the woman will bruise my head." So Cain and Abel were born, and the devil tried to destroy the seed.

The devil must have tried to persuade both Cain and Abel. "You don't both have to obey God… did He say bring the first fruit?"

Cain fell for it, but Abel stood in his resolve and he remembered the teachings of his father. He said, "No, that is not what I was taught to do. I was taught that the first belongs to God, the best belongs to God, and so I am giving God the best."

Because the Seed of Righteousness was in Abel, the devil thought, "This must be it, because this is the one that I have failed to bring to my side." So the devil got into Cain and caused him to slay Abel. Notice the devil did not destroy Cain. Cain was the lesser one, there was already evil in him; two cannot walk together unless they are in agreement.

What the devil failed to do with Cain, he tried again and again in so many different adventures in the Word of God. For example, when the children of Israel began to multiply and become so many, Pharaoh was intimidated; he was afraid that they might become a mighty army. So what did he do? And who was behind it?

IN THE FULLNESS OF TIME

But when the fullness of time had come, God sent forth His Son, born of a woman, born under the Law.

(Galatians 4:4)

It is important to understand that God does not move before time, and He does not move after time. He moves at the right time, in the fullness of time. This also means that if your timing is off, and you miss God, you miss Him utterly.

In the fullness of time, the Seed became a "He," uppercase "H." "He," denoting deity, power, dominion, authority: the Seed became "He" in the fullness of time.

THE ANGEL'S ANNOUNCEMENT

In the fullness of time, God sent His Son, born of a woman according to the Law, and the angel went to Mary.

When Gabriel announced himself to Mary, he said, "I am Gabriel, for I stand before the Lord." There are different categories of angels; not every angel stands before God. In other words, not every angel has the privilege to stand in the presence of the Lord. "I hear directly from God and God has sent me to you with a message. Hail Mary! Thou are blessed and favored among women."

Mary was frightened just by the very presence of Heaven, and wondered, "What is this?"

The angel continued with the announcement that she would conceive in her womb and bring forth a Son, and His name would be called Jesus, for He would be the Savior of this world.

But before all of that happened, Isaiah the prophet, in fact, all of the prophets, announced it. Isaiah in particular is known as the Messianic Prophet. He announced in Isaiah 7:14, *"the virgin shall conceive, and bear a Son, and shall call his name Immanuel."* Immanuel: God with us, in other words, God will come and make His abode among men, within men.

THE SEED TO PREPARE THE WAY

Elizabeth, the cousin of Mary, was known as "barren"; she had no child and had reached old age. She longed for a child, but that child would not come until the fullness of time.

God works according to revelatory time; He does not just work for the sake of working. God will not move just because He wants to make you happy, God will move because it is beneficial to His Kingdom.

You need to understand that Elizabeth remained barren until the fullness of time because Mary had not yet been born. There is no way that Elizabeth would have become pregnant if Mary was not on the scene, because the purpose of Elizabeth becoming pregnant was to bring forth the seed who was John the Baptist, who was ordained to prepare the way. So Elizabeth had to remain barren until Mary was born.

Once Mary was born, Elizabeth took seed six months before Mary did, six being the number of human completion.

The Bible tells us that Elizabeth hid in the hill country while she was pregnant. Meanwhile, the angel visited Mary, and said, "Hail Mary, you are blessed and highly favored."

In other words, "You are the chosen one. It has pleased Him to choose you to bring forth the Seed that will tread on the head of the enemy."

A PURE VESSEL

The devil is a fool. I do not know why he thought for even one moment that God would use Eve to bring forth the Seed, because Eve was already beguiled, she was defiled, and God could not use a defiled vessel to bring forth a righteous Seed. The vessel had to be clean, the vessel had to be pure, because the Seed was a pure Seed, the Seed was God Himself.

If your body is defiled you cannot carry the anointing.

Mary said to the angel, "Now how can these things be? I know not a man." He replied that the Holy Ghost, the power of the Highest, would overshadow her. And it was so, and Mary conceived.

When Mary conceived, the Bible says she also went over to the hill country. She was impregnated with the Seed that would destroy the head of the serpent.

When the seed inside of Elizabeth came into the presence of Mary, the chosen vessel of the Seed that would bruise the head of the serpent, Scripture says,

And it happened, when Elizabeth heard the greeting of Mary, that the babe leaped in her womb; and Elizabeth was filled with the Holy Spirit.
(Luke 1:41)

JESUS IS THE SEED

We know the Seed is Jesus, but who is Jesus?

In the beginning was the Word, and the Word was with God, and the Word was God. He was in the beginning with God. All things were made through Him, and without Him nothing was made that was made. In Him was life, and the life was the light of men. And the light shines in the darkness, and the darkness did not comprehend it.
(John 1:1-5)

Jesus is the Word, and He is our light. In other words, the prophetic, which is Jesus, which is the Word that is in your belly, is the Light that will shine in your darkness.

The Seed became flesh, the Seed named Immanuel, and dwelt among us, and we beheld His glory, the glory of the only Begotten of the Father, full of grace and truth.

CHAPTER THREE

Armed and Dangerous

What then is a Seed? The dictionary defines "seed" as "a source or beginning." The Seed, Jesus, is the source of our power over the enemy.

Although Jesus is not physically here now, in the flesh with you and I, the Bible says, *"In the beginning was the Word, and the Word was with God"* (John 1:1). *"And the Word became flesh and dwelt among us"* (John 1:14).

FILL YOUR BELLY WITH THE WORD

When the Word is released and you conceive the Word in your belly; when the Word is spoken and dispersed, and your belly conceives the Word, you are armed and dangerous. But until you have a revelation of what you are carrying in your belly, you do not have the potency or the power to bruise the head of the serpent.

This is why you must go to your Bible, go to the Word, eat the Word. Be like Ezekiel: take the scroll, eat the Word, fill your belly!

Don't Miss It!

The tragedy is that this generation has missed it. There are people that God has raised in this last hour who are pregnant with the Word, as Mary was pregnant. But they are unaware, and the Seed lies dormant within them.

Jesus was sent to deliver, to save, to heal, to set the captives free. Mary was pregnant with deliverance, she was pregnant with Salvation, she was pregnant with power, she was pregnant with joy, she was pregnant with a powerful anointing. It was all in her belly.

Don't Shut Him Out!

When the fullness of time came for Mary to give birth, she went from one hotel to another, knocking at the door, "Have you got any room for me? I am carrying what you need, I am carrying your next deliverance, I am carrying your next healing, I am carrying your next level, is there any room for me?"

But they said, "There is no room here!" The religious folks, the traditional folks shut her out. They all shut their doors, and they said, "We do not have room for that nonsense, we have no room for all of that, what are you carrying anyway?"

Someone Needs What You Have

They all shut their doors, but Mary said, "Don't worry about it."

And Joseph said, "Don't worry about it. We are going to give birth to this baby wherever we can. We will give birth because there's somebody out there who needs it."

And there is someone out there who needs what you have. There is somebody out there who needs the power in your belly, the salvation that you are carrying. There is someone who needs the miracle - it may not take place in a church, it may not be from the pulpit, you may not have a microphone - but there is someone who needs what you have.

OPEN THE DOOR!

So Mary went to the manger, to the lowest place where the animals were, and she knocked and said, "Is there any room here?"

And the cows, the donkeys, the lambs said, "Come on in."

The camel said, "Come on in! We don't have a lot to offer, but come on in."

Similarly, Jesus seeks to enter our lives. He said, "Behold, I stand at the door and knock. If anyone hears My voice and opens the door, I will come in to him and dine with him, and he with Me" (Revelation 3:20).

Mary went in and she gave birth to the salvation of the entire world. She gave birth to the Seed that will destroy the head of the serpent.

When Mary gave birth, the angels of the Lord went out to the shepherds tending their flocks by night. Then the shepherds began to announce, "Today in the city of David a Savior has been born, an anointing has been delivered."

And today, right where you are, an anointing has been born. There is power, there is an anointing, there is glory within your belly!

FOLLOW THE STAR

The shepherds began to follow the star to the City of David, looking for the next king, the King of the Jews, the King of all the others; looking for the Seed of the woman that will bruise the head of the serpent.

In another part of the town there were three wise men who also saw the Star of David. They had read in the Old Testament that a star would rise, and that this star would signify the birth of the Savior, the Messiah, the Seed that will bruise the head of the serpent. So they began to follow the Star.

WISE MEN FOLLOW JESUS

It is only the wise who follow Jesus, only the wise who follow the truth. The foolish cannot follow Jesus, they cannot see the truth. "For the message of the cross is foolishness to those who are perishing, but to us who are being saved it is the power of God" (1 Corinthians 1:18).

So the wise men followed the Star and arrived in Jerusalem. They stood before King Herod and announced that they were looking for the King who had been born.

Troubled, Herod asked, "Who is He that has been born King of the Jews?"

Because, you see, the devil was in Herod, thinking, "This must be the Seed that is going to bruise my head!"

So Herod said to the wise men, "Go and look for Him that I to may come and serve Him." Of course, the devil had no intention of serving the Seed; the devil intended to kill the Seed before its time.

Don't Come Empty-Handed

When the wise men went looking for the Seed of the woman that would bruise the head of the serpent, they did not go empty-handed. They were going to look for a King; He was in a cradle, but He was a King. He was a baby, but He was a King. So when the wise men went, the Bible specifies three of them, but there could have been more, they went with gold, frankincense and myrrh.

When you receive a revelation that you are going to receive your portion, your impartation of the Seed which is the Word, your deposit of the Word that will destroy your particular serpent, you cannot afford to go empty-handed. You must bring your humility, your willingness, your obedience.

Bow Before the King

The wise men took gold, frankincense and myrrh, and they bowed down before the King lying in the manger.

And when they bowed, they were not really just bowing before the King, but they were bowing before the Seed. They were bowing before their answer; they were bowing before the Word that was going to be deposited in their belly, the Word that was going to crush the head of the serpent that had come against their families, against their finances, against their businesses.

They bowed down and they worshipped, and they presented their gifts before the Seed. They opened their gifts before Him and they worshipped.

That night when they began their journey back, the Lord visited them. He gave them a vision and said, "Do not return the same way that you came because Herod is waiting for you."

RECEIVE THE SEED!

Many of you need a deposit of the Word, a Seed in your belly that will destroy the devil. Satan has been on your back and you need some direction.

Some of you may not be sick in your body or have a tumor in your breast; you may not have a problem at all - you simply need a visitation from God, some direction. All you need is instruction.

Just as the wise men received direction from the Lord and returned by a different path, when you begin to heed the Seed that is in you, you will not be the same. Your direction will change.

Tell the Lord right now: "I need direction. I need a visitation from You, Jesus. I come before You now to receive a deposit of the Seed that will destroy the head of the serpent that is in my home, that has infiltrated my children, that has attacked my finances, that has come against my business, my ministry."

Open up your spiritual womb and receive the Seed, the incorruptible Seed that has power to destroy every yoke, to loose the bondage of the enemy; the Seed which is the Word.

CHAPTER FOUR

Walk in Obedience

BUILD ON THE ROCK

When Peter said to Jesus, *"Thou art the Christ, the Son of the living God"* (Matthew 16:16, KJV), Jesus was overwhelmed, He was excited. Someone had finally tapped into the secret wherein they ought to build!

So Jesus responded with a powerful statement,

> *Blessed are you, Simon Bar-Jonah, for flesh and blood has not revealed this to you, but My Father who is in Heaven...and on this rock I will build My church, and the gates of Hades shall not prevail against it.*
>
> (Matthew 16:17-18)

JESUS WAS DESCRIBING THE ROCK OF REVELATION.

Everything that you build upon the rock of revelation will stand. You cannot build successfully on just any kind of foundation. Simply because someone else had a plan that worked for them does not mean it will work for you. You must have a personal revelation, and it is the rock of this personal revelation that will cause whatever you are building to stand.

So we are going to receive the revelation of God's Word, and upon that revelation we are going to be able to build and to stand against the onset of the enemy, and through that revelation God will take us to new dimensions in Him.

GOING INTO HIDING

Previously we learned that the enemy went to the woman in the garden and deceived and beguiled her to disobey the Word of God. Then God came walking into the garden, looking for Adam and Eve.

Every time you disobey God, you go into hiding! Every time you walk in disobedience, your flesh has a tendency to hide.

Remember when you used to jump out of the window and sneak off to parties? Afterwards, you began creeping back; hoping that your parents were asleep and would not catch you. But the moment you crept back, they met you at the door.

All of a sudden you do not want to come out of your room anymore; you do not want to come down for lunch, you do not want to come out for dinner. You find yourself hiding all the time, confined to your room, because you disobeyed, you broke a law, you stepped into a zone that you were not meant to step into.

Sin always makes us hide.

But we cannot hide from God.

An Appointment with God

So God walked in the cool of the garden, waiting, looking for Adam and Eve.

"Adam, where are you? You are not at the place that I normally find you. There is that place where you and I meet consistently, but you are not there."

It is imperative that you have a place of communion with God, where you meet Him on a consistent basis.

Every morning when we arrive at 5:00 a.m., we have purposed to meet God. He knows that He has an appointment with us at 5:00 a.m. Tuesday through Friday, so every morning He is waiting for us to show up.

God had an appointment time when He normally came into the Garden and communed with Adam and with Eve, but that particular day when God came, He could not find them. The enemy had deceived the woman to eat of the forbidden fruit and she had given some to her husband, and he too had eaten thereof. So they were in hiding, not in their place of communion.

The First Gospel

The first promise given after Adam and Eve ate the forbidden fruit in the Garden of Eden is also the first

Gospel sermon ever preached on the face of the earth. Theologians call it the Proto-Evangelion, which simply means the first Gospel.

"He shall bruise your head, and you shall bruise His heel" (Genesis 3:15). These words spoken by God contain the earliest promise of redemption in the Bible, and everything else in Scripture flows from this one verse. It is a principle Scripture.

The devil thought he had corrupted God's creation, that it was over for them, and indeed it was over for them at a certain level because death entered the picture and Adam and Eve were asked to leave the Garden. But God had another plan.

OVERTURNING THE CURSE

Some may be tempted to discount the first 11 chapters of Genesis because it may seem they have nothing to do with Christ, but that is not true. Jesus came to overturn the curse of Genesis Chapter Three, and that we may know that which has been freely given unto us. *"Christ has redeemed us from the curse of the law, having become a curse for us* (for it is written, 'Cursed is everyone who hangs on a tree'), *that the blessing of Abraham might come upon the Gentiles"* (Galatians 3:13).

The curse that was released in Genesis Chapter Three is the reason Jesus, the last Adam, was sent. Therefore we cannot ignore the clear teaching of the opening chapters of the Bible if we hope to understand the true meaning of the entire message of salvation.

So although you may not see it at first glance, Christ is in Genesis 3:15. He is the ultimate Seed of the woman who would one day come to crush the serpent's ugly head. In the process His heel would be bruised and His body would be broken on the cross.

In short, this verse predicts that Jesus would win the victory over Satan, but would Himself be wounded in the process.

THE BRUISED HEEL

One of the principles of battle, one of the dynamics, is that sometimes when you are at war with the enemy, you get wounded. You may win the battle, but you come out of it with cuts and bruises. When your opponent hits you, gives you a black eye, you still get up and hit him back. He buckles up and gets up and you hit him again. At the end, you win the battle. Still, you leave the battleground with a few bruises, a black eye, a cut lip; but you won!

God said, "He will bruise your heel, but you will bruise his head."

It has been scientifically proven that nobody has died from a bruised heal. You may limp a little bit, but it will not kill you. The devil will hit you, but remember what Paul wrote,

We are hard-pressed on every side, yet not crushed; we are perplexed, but not in despair; persecuted, but not forsaken; struck down, but not destroyed.
(2 Corinthians 4:8-9)

You may be hit from every side, nevertheless you still have some power in you; you may be bruised, but you are not totally destroyed.

BRUISE THE HEAD!

So you will find in the course of battle that you will get wounded, you will get bruised, you will get hurt, but you need to understand that the Seed of the woman, the Seed which is the Word, the Seed which is Jesus, is in your belly and no matter what the devil does to bruise your heel, you still have the power to take the Seed, which is the Word, and bruise the head.

THE BLAME GAME

So we read that at the beginning of human history, Adam and Eve ate the prohibited produce, sin entered paradise, and their first impulse was to hide from God.

Their second impulse was to make excuses for their sin. Adam blamed the woman and Eve blamed the serpent. No one was willing to get up and say, "I did it."

No one was willing to stand up and take responsibility, does that not sound like today? No one is ready to take responsibility for everything that is going on; for the sin that is rampant in our world.

Think about this: Adam blamed the woman... but in reality, Adam was blaming God. He was saying, "It is her fault, that woman You gave me. I did not ask for her; You gave her to me. I did not tell you that I wasn't good being alone."

LIVING IN THE SPIRIT

But the Word is clear: God saw that it was not good for Adam to be alone. The Bible does not say that Adam saw. In other words, Adam never went to God, he never murmured, he never complained. He was happy having dominion, managing, being a steward of the Garden, having rule and dominion over the animals, telling the donkey to do this, telling the rock to move there. Adam was happy with what he was doing, but it was God that saw that it was not good that man should be alone. Adam, even though he was a spirit being, lived in a body made of flesh.

And though Adam did not know it, we know that man cannot be in the spirit 24 hours a day, 7 days a week. After we preach, cast out devils, guess what? The body says, "I need some water." Our flesh needs relief.

Most of us cannot be so anointed to a point where we say, "I'm in the spirit," and that is it. We spend good parts of the day in the flesh as well.

I do know some holy ones of Israel, who, when you try to talk to them, speak back to you in tongues, and you cannot get a single word of English out of them, because they are frequently in the spirit.

But when you are that heavenly minded, you are no earthly good.

41

And there are others who are so earthly minded that they are no heavenly good. God wanted there to be a balance.

So God said that it was not good that man should be alone, and He gave him Eve. She was beguiled, they hid, God looked for them, and Adam blamed God and said, "It was that woman you gave me, it was her fault."

Then the woman blamed the serpent and said, "It was the serpent who gave me the apple to eat."

The blame game did not begin yesterday; it began way back in the Garden of Eden.

And so now you understand why every time something goes wrong, the husband blames the wife; the wife blames the husband. "Where are my socks; where is my dinner? Why is there no hot water?" It all began with Adam and Eve.

CHAPTER FIVE

Paradise Lost?

God came in after Adam and Eve had eaten, and their eyes were opened. Suddenly, it was not so beautiful; the entrance of sin had ruined Eden. Dark shadows fell on the ground as they contemplated what they had done. The smell of death was in the air.

Under a nearby tree, the serpent lay quietly, alone, delighting in the events of the day. This was his plan from the very beginning. He had intended to humiliate God by ruining paradise, and now it appeared he had done so. He had shown the whole universe that God's great experiment could not work, that no race of beings could ever be trusted to freely obey God; left to themselves they would always disobey, even in paradise.

JUDGMENT DELIVERED

As God surveyed the moral wreckage of the Fall, He immediately began to deliver the judgment. He began where the sin began, with the serpent.

For that reason you need to be careful that you are not an instigator like the serpent. Do not start trouble; because God is not going to deal with the ones who followed you, He is going to deal with the one who started it - you.

Do not ever start anything, do not influence people negatively, do not sow seeds of discord.

Personally, I have always been careful; out of all the seven children my mother had, she always told me that I was the one child that never gave her trouble. Not that I did not have the capacity to, I sure did, but there was just something within me that always observed a red light: "Don't do that; don't go there."

It is my resolve in my spirit to refuse to walk under a curse.

THE WAY OF OBEDIENCE

Many years ago when I had finished my A level and was waiting for the results before I went on to university, my girlfriend and I saw an ad in the paper to be airline hostesses. As young girls, we were excited; we wanted to travel the world. We qualified because all they required was that we be tall, slim, and have the "walk." My girlfriend said, "Sarah, don't you think that would be wonderful?"

I said, "Now Rose, do you think I've got the walk?"

She said, "Oh yeah!"

So we said, "Let's go for it!" We went and got the application forms and filled them all in. We could not wait to see the world, we were so excited.

Then I took my application form to my dad. I said, "Dad, look, we are going to travel the world! Isn't this exciting, isn't this wonderful?"

My dad looked at me and said, "Isn't this what?"

I continued, "Dad, can you imagine what it will be like? I am going to go to Japan, to Tokyo, to England; I'll be traveling the world! Can you imagine all the nice things I'll be able to bring back?"

He said, "Nice things, what? No. Not one of my children will go down to that level."

For whatever reason, my dad did not approve of me being a stewardess. He said that stewardesses travel the world, with a man in every port: a boyfriend in Japan, a boyfriend in Hong Kong.

So he said, "Not out of this house." And then he made a statement that really gave me chills. He said, "If you choose to go that way, when I die, do not come to my funeral."

I was not a Christian back then; I was just a churchgoer. My mother was born-again, tongue-talking, spirit-filled, but I was not a Christian - I had not given my heart to the Lord yet. But I knew something about obedience to your parents, and I knew the consequences of disobedience, and as a result a fear gripped my heart and I threw my application out.

45

THE WAY OF SIN

The next day I met my friend, Rose, and she was ready to turn in those applications. But I said, "I am not going."

She said, "What is wrong with you? You are always that way, spoiling stuff! Come on, let's go do it!"

She almost persuaded me. But at the last minute, I got out. I was just too afraid to die!

Sometimes you have to be afraid to die; because there are some things you do that will kill you before your time.

Sin will take you further than you want to go, it will keep you longer than you want to stay, and it will make you pay more than you want to pay.

And so I said, "No, Rose, I'm not going that route. If you want to go, you go ahead."

To make a long story short, I obeyed my Dad because I did not want to walk under a curse. This has been my resolve all my life, even to the point of getting down on my knees and making peace with somebody. I just refuse to live under a curse, and I do not want my Seed to live under a curse.

I tore my application form up, but Rose went ahead and became a stewardess. And I am sad to say, she is dead now. Many, many times I prayed for her. Many, many times the Spirit of God brought her into my dreams, but she is dead.

Sin will kill you, disobedience will kill you, before your time.

46

HE HAS NO FAVORITES

If God does not fulfill His Word, then He is not God. But He is God. And God has no favorites.

David was the apple of God's eye. He was the sweet Psalmist of Israel. God loved David. He was a worshipper; he was a man that knew how to get to the heart of God. But David stepped out of line with God. He went for Bathsheba, killed her husband, and then tried to manipulate God with fasting and prayer.

But fasting and prayer cannot manipulate God.

Your fasting and prayer will not manipulate God. You do not twist the hand of God just because you are fasting and praying.

God loved David, but David disobeyed Him. On top of that, David was a king. In other words, God said, "You are My reflection and the world is looking at you. If I do not judge you, that encourages everyone to do what you did and get away with it."

Still, David began to fast and pray, "O God, please don't kill my seed, don't kill the seed with Bathsheba."

For seven days he fasted and prayed, but the more he fasted, the worse the child became.

Finally, while he was still lying out, fasting, his servant came and said, "The child is dead. Get up, wash yourself and eat bread, for the child is dead. The thing that you have brought out of sin is dead."

47

God will not tolerate sin, no matter how much He loves you. He does not play favorites.

Expand Your Horizons

The Bible says, "...by the mouth of two or three witnesses the matter shall be established" (Deuteronomy 19:15). In other words, do not just take one Scripture; take the time to find the Scriptures that cross-reference with the passage that you are studying.

That is how the devil tries to fool us; he gives us half a Scripture, or a single Scripture taken out of context. When Satan tempted Jesus, that is what he did, but because Jesus knew the full Scripture, Satan was defeated.

The Curse Will Come Full Circle

When you choose to walk under a curse, understand that it will eventually come full circle. If it does not hit you, it will hit the third, fourth, even fifth generations.

Seeing the curse, you may wonder, "What is going on? I served God, everything was wonderful."

But God will say, "Oh no, remember when you chose not to obey? This is merely the result of your disobedience." Just as He told David, "As a consequence, I am going to cause people to rape your wife. I am going to cause people to commit adultery with her."

The curse will go full circle unless you choose to humble yourself and walk in obedience. As Paul said, sometimes you must be foolish to be wise. Even if you know you are right, sometimes you need to be a fool to be wise.

You are willing to be a fool because you know what you are looking for, you know where you are going, you know what God has for you.

THE FEUD BEGINS

So Adam and Eve disobeyed and hid from God. God came looking for them and pronounced the curse. Let us now return to Genesis 3:15 to discover what the curse predicts for Satan, for Christ and for us. We may summarize this passage's predictive teaching as follows: there will be an endless conflict.

God said,

And I will put enmity between you and the woman,
and between your offspring and hers.
(Genesis 3:15, NIV)

The key word is "enmity," which means hostility or animosity. One translation says, "I will set a feud," and another puts it this way: "there will be a war." The New Living Translation says, "You and the woman will be enemies."

WATCH OUT FOR WOMEN

You, the devil and the woman will be enemies. For this reason, women are more aggressive with the devil.

49

Let your wife find a "Delilah" near you, and you will see her wrath. She will take her hammer and smash the head of the devil.

Many men do not understand women's innate aggressiveness. They have a tendency to wonder why women become so jealous and act foolish. Men, you must recognize there was a war announced between the devil and the woman, and this war continues to this day.

Every time a demon tries to mess with your marriage, there is something that rises up, that comes from Genesis 3:15, and says, "The war is on, Baby! Whatever you touch, God has given me the power to bruise your head."

DON'T TOUCH HER SEED

Just let the devil try and touch the seed of a woman, try and touch her child. Say she receives a report that another child scratched her child. Immediately she will go and look for that child and its mother, and she will get up in their faces, saying, "How dare you touch my child; how dare you touch my seed! Don't you know that that is my child?" Even though she may know that her child is in the wrong, she will defend her seed, because the war started in Genesis 3:15.

God pronounced judgment, a conflict, war. He pronounced it and said, "From this day forward, I have declared war." God declared war between the serpent and the woman, between the seed of the woman and the seed of the serpent: the posterity, the offspring, the generations that were yet unborn that were going to come forth out of the womb of the serpent and out of the womb of the woman.

God said there will consistently be war. There will be war between light and darkness, between truth and error, between flesh and the spirit. He declared war upon the enemy, so Eve and the serpent will never get along.

CHAPTER SIX

The Devil is Not Your Friend

RECOGNIZE THE DEVIL IN ALL HIS GUISES

The devil has never changed. He masquerades as an angel of light, so you must have the spirit of discernment. Understand that everyone who cries, "Jesus, Jesus" is not for the Lord. Not everyone clapping their hands and dancing, lifting up their hands and falling on the floor is for the Lord. You need to know the Spirit to be able to discern what is of God and what is of the devil.

The Bible says the serpent was the most subtle among all the creatures. Serpents are beautiful to look at; their skin glitters. Look at how many people spend hundreds of dollars buying snakeskin shoes, because they are beautiful, they glitter, they shine.

The devil is not your friend. I do not care in what shape, what color or what form he appears, he is not your friend.

You may come dressed up, looking all wonderful from the crown of your head to the top of your feet, but if I see the seed of the devil in you, I have no friendship with you.

That is how the devil deceives us; we look at the outward without taking the time to look on the inside.

THE PRIDE THAT GOETH BEFORE THE FALL

Before God created this earth, there was a previous earth: this is called the antediluvian age. In Ezekiel 28, God is angry with Lucifer, the "morning star." He says, *"You were in Eden"* (Ezekiel 28:13), in other words, "You were in the first Eden, before you defiled it and it was destroyed."

The Bible says of Satan, *"your heart was lifted up"* (Ezekiel 28:17) and *"you have set your heart as the heart of a god"* (Ezekiel 28:6). Satan wanted to be like God. He did not want to praise God anymore, he wanted to be praised; he did not want to worship anymore, he wanted to be worshiped. He was full of pride. So Satan rebelled against God.

Do not let the spirit of pride overtake you, because pride is the one spirit that will lead to a fall. I do not care who you are, the moment pride hits, get ready to fall.

It is the devil that puts pride in your spirit, saying, "Who do they think they are, telling you that?"

Watch out for those voices that pump you up, that make you think, "I'm all that." Those are the voices of the enemy, who would be delighted to plant a seed of pride in

you whereby you will think that you are better than everyone else and without you nothing can happen. He wants
you to think that the whole world revolves around you.

But remember, the devil is a liar!

GENERATION AFTER GENERATION

The devil was kicked out of Heaven and gained access
to Earth.

> *A great, fiery red dragon...drew a third of the stars*
> *of Heaven and threw them to the earth.*
> (Revelation 12:3-4)

> *Then I heard a loud voice saying in Heaven,*
> *'...Woe to the inhabitants of the earth and the sea!*
> *For the devil has come down to you, having great*
> *wrath, because he knows that he has a short time.'*
> (Revelation 12:10, 12)

So God pronounced the judgment, saying that there
will be enmity, not just between the woman and the devil,
but between their seed, their offspring, their posterity, all
the generations that are yet unborn. There will always be
a conflict, there will always be enmity, there will always
be a fight between Satan and the woman.

THE GODLY SEED

The "seed" ultimately refers to the men and the women
of faith in every generation who have believed in God;
they are the seed of the woman. The godly line of Abel,
Enoch, Noah, Abraham, Isaac, Jacob, Joseph, Moses,

Joshua, Gideon, David, Daniel and the rest - those were the seed of the woman that God used in different generations.

THE SEED OF SATAN

It is obvious that Satan has his seed too, because throughout history in every generation, in every country, in every city, in every village, in every tribe and clan, and even in many families, Satan has had his people.

The seed of the devil is poverty, sickness, infirmity, plague, epidemics, lack, insufficiency. Through his seed Satan tries to quench, to abort, to cause God's seed to miscarry. He uses infirmity, sickness, poverty.

When you struggle to pay your bills, your car note, your house note, it is the result of the seed of the devil contesting with the Seed of God that is in you.

That sinful seed began with Cain, who killed Abel, and continued through the wicked generation of Noah's day, to the Pharaoh who opposed Moses, to the Canaanites who mugged Joshua. The Canaanites, the Amalekites, Pharaoh and Herod were all seeds of the enemy, positioned to bruise the heel of the Seed of the woman.

TRIPPING AND FALLING

Why is it that so many Christians stumble? Because the enemy has bruised their heels.

Every time you stumble, the serpent has bit your heel with unforgiveness or anger or animosity. Perhaps you are waiting for something that has not happened, and suddenly you get an attitude. So you decide you do not want to pay your tithe because you are angry with God. Guess what? That is Satan causing you to stumble.

Do not allow Satan to cause you to fall! Your seed is the Word of God; use it to bruise the head of the serpent.

It is important for you to understand that you bruise Satan's head because without the head, the body cannot function. When your heel is bruised, on the other hand, you limp a little bit, but you can still walk, you can still function. You can still fight the enemy.

THE HEAD NOT THE HEEL

God specifically instructed that the Seed of the woman would bruise the head of the serpent, and the serpent would strike the heel of the Seed of the woman. The word "head" here in the Hebrew rendering is the word "ro'sh," as in the head of the human body, the head of a line, what is principle or supreme, that which is first, that which is top, that which is praised, the highest part, the summit, the beginning, the foremost, the leader and the chief.

Just as we have the head of a company, the head of a home, the head of a business; here the Bible is referring to its chief person, and so "ro'sh" is used to show leadership, headship. The promise is that the Seed of the woman would someday crush the serpent's head, its headship. The woman in particular would play a part in undoing the effects of the fall of humanity. The head must be bruised because it is principle, it is supreme, it is the top. And when you bruise the head, the entire body becomes ineffective.

TOTAL DESTRUCTION

So God was specific when He released His judgment and said that the Seed of the woman will bruise, will crush the head of the seed of the serpent. In other words, "totally destroy."

All the offspring of the devil may come against you: barrenness, lack, sickness, poverty, but the purpose of this book is to equip you to be able to overcome. You are powerful! You may not know how powerful you are, but God is unfolding this mystery to the Body of Christ. You do not have to be poor; you do not have to tolerate sickness, because dominion power, Kingdom power, is in your belly.

CHAPTER SEVEN

Bringing the Seed to Fruition

"The seed is the Word of God" (Luke 8:11).

The Word is a Seed, but even Jesus, who is the Word, had to be quickened. The Word went to John the Baptist, who baptized Him. The Word came up praying, the heavens were opened, the Spirit of the Lord descended in the bodily form of a dove and sat upon the Word, the voice of God began to speak and the Word was quickened.

Tell the enemy, "Do not play with me, I am not who you think I am. I am a time bomb ready to explode; I am just waiting to be quickened."

GOD DOESN'T FIGHT FAIR

And I will put enmity between you and the woman, and between your seed and her Seed; He shall bruise your head, and you shall bruise His heel.
(Genesis 3:15)

Let us look at the key words that were used in this particular passage of Scripture. God gave the Seed of the woman divine permission to strike the head, but gave the serpent limited power to strike only the heel.

In other words, God doesn't fight fair. God made this war a mismatch. It is similar to a fight between a light weight and a heavy weight.

God said, "Devil, you are forever under My seat. You will never assume the role and the authority that I have as God. I will continue to let you know that I am indeed the Sovereign Ruler of the universe."

OUR SIDE WINS!

You must understand that when you are a child of God you are always on the winning side. For example, you go for a job interview although you know you do not have the qualifications. There are several people lined up who do qualify for the job. They have their diplomas, they have the experience, and you have nothing. But all of a sudden, guess who they select? They select you, because though others had more qualifications, you had more God.

God let the devil know that it did not matter what he had done, God is still God. He is still the Eternal, He still has authority and He will not allow this to be a fair fight. "You may strike the heel of my servant, but your head will be smitten by the Seed of the woman."

DAVID VERSUS GOLIATH

Goliath stood nine feet tall with armor all over; he was a trained soldier. Israel had tried for many days, but they could not get rid of Goliath. Then came little David, anointed and appointed by God, and all he had was a sling and a stone.

When David looked at Goliath with his tall body, his armor, his experience, all his weapons, he must have said, "O my God, what am I going to do?"

But no matter how big, how great, how awesome the enemy looks, if your God is bigger than the enemy, then God is going to bring that enemy down!

God was on the side of David, he had more God than Goliath had. All you need is more God. A wonderful house, a beautiful car, money in the bank do not mean anything when God is on your side.

"If God is for us, who can be against us" (Romans 8:31)?

WATCH WHO YOU FIGHT

It is important that you do not come against people that have "a lot of God." God will go to war for His own with everything that He has.

Moses went to Pharaoh and said, "God, I Am that I Am, sent me; set the people of God free." Pharaoh tried to oppose him, but God lifted up a battle with Pharaoh.

Do not touch anybody that has God on their side! If they have more God than you, you had better step back, because God will cause a storm!

You need to know who you are fighting.

The Bible says,

He reproved kings for their sakes; saying, 'Touch not Mine anointed, and do My prophets no harm.'
(Psalm 105:14-15)

Do not mess with a man that is full of God, with a woman that goes before God, consistently praying and calling on the name of the Lord. God Himself will come down and deal with the issue. You may think you are winning for a while, but if that prophet is full of God, he has more God than you have brains, he has more God than you have a degree, he has more God than you have money, and God will fight for him.

Aaron and Miriam rose up against Moses; God said, "I know that you are a prophetess, Miriam. I know you are anointed, I know you bang the tambourine, I know you are gifted, but let Me tell you something, the man that you are up against has got more of Me."

It is not going to be a fair fight. "I have given the seed of the woman authority to bruise your head, Satan; to crush your head. And once your head is bruised, than your entire body is of no effect."

Who can fight God and win?

GET MORE GOD

For this reason you need to seek God with all of your heart, to spend time praying and fasting, to spend time calling on the name of the Lord. God will come out full force for you. All you need to do is seek more of God

Those of you who are looking for husbands, it is great to have all of your wonderful makeup, to do your hair, to get your facial, but you will still need more God. Your long legs and good looks are not going to get you the man you are looking for. If they do, he might not be the right man, because after a time, the flower will fade and the grass will wither, especially after you have had a few babies. And if those long legs are gone, your man might be gone as well. So you had better be sure that you got into that marriage with God, because if God got you into it, God will keep you there.

IT DOESN'T MATTER WHO
WINS THE BEAUTY PAGEANT

Esther looked at all of the beautiful virgins vying for the king and said, "I know you have the wonderful skin tone, I know your hair is gorgeous, but I am going into the king's palace because I have more God." And she was right.

Before my husband and I got married, I used to go to church and see women in all shapes, colors and sizes sashaying up to him. They showed up with all kinds of outfits and colognes, the light-skinned, the brown, the red, all with immaculate hair. All of them were parading, everybody showing what they had, strutting their stuff.

The whole time, I simply went to God. I said, "God, if it be Your will, let it come to pass. I can't compete; look at how wonderful they look, how glorious. Look at their color, their hair, their style, their clothes. God, I am nothing, but I know that if You be for me, who can be against me?" And amazingly, when the pageant was over, I had won.

GOD WILL GET YOU THROUGH

God will take you through the storm, He will take you under, He will take you over, He will take you around. God will take you through all the seasons of your life.

No weapon that is formed against you shall prosper; every tongue that rises up against you in judgment, you have the power to condemn.

THE DEVIL DOESN'T HAVE A CHANCE

God did not even give the devil a chance. If God was fair, He would have told the devil, "I give you both the same opportunity, you crush his head, and you crush her head." But He did not.

The battle between light and darkness is not a fair fight.

The battle between life and death is not a fair fight.

The greater one, the one with more authority, will always win the battle.

GOD IS A RESPECTER OF PRINCIPLES

Unfortunately, the Church today has come to a place where everybody is right in their own eyes. But God is no respecter of persons; God is a respecter of principles. If you step out of line with God, it does not matter who you are.

God wanted the devil to know He was taking up the battle because the Seed of the woman was God Himself incarnate. "Because of what you did to My creation, I am taking up this battle."

If you have more God, God will make things happen. People will look at you funny and say, "How did you do that, how did that happen for you?" It happened not because of who you are, but because of what you stand for.

ONCE A LIAR, ALWAYS A LIAR

Why do you not understand My speech? Because you are not able to listen to My Word.
(John 8:43)

Every time there is a lack of understanding, every time there is an inability to comprehend and to understand, there is a spirit that has taken a hold of you. Satan will use every opportunity to confuse and confound God's people.

The seed of the devil lies; he has no truth in him. He lied from the beginning, in Genesis 3:15, when he went and deceived the woman.

You are of your father the devil, and the desires of your father you want to do. He was a murderer from the beginning, and does not stand in the truth, because there is no truth in him. When he speaks a lie, he speaks from his own resources, for he is a liar and the father of it (John 8:44)

Jesus was speaking to these people, the Pharisees, because they were the seed of the serpent.

Anyone who rises up against the Seed of the woman is the seed of the serpent.

So Jesus addressed them, saying, "Because you do not understand Me and you are rising up against Me, I know who you are. I recognize you; you are the seed of the serpent who was in the garden, who beguiled the woman."

THE ENEMIES OF RIGHTEOUSNESS

But Elymas the sorcerer (for so his name is translated) withstood them, seeking to turn the proconsul away from the faith.

(Acts 13:8)

Elymas was a sorcerer. Sorcery is a direct seed of the devil. Many people think that sorcery or divination is when you sit down and burn a candle, or get on a broom. The Bible, however, says that rebellion is at the seat of witchcraft. As a matter of fact, rebellion is witchcraft; disobedience is witchcraft.

Here we are seeing some of the seeds of the enemy. Elymas, the sorcerer, withstands those who are standing for God, and he seeks to turn the proconsul away from the faith.

> *Then Saul, who also is called Paul, filled with the Holy Spirit, looked intently at him and said, 'O full of all deceit and all fraud, you son of the devil.'*
> (Acts 13:9-10)

Another translation says "you seed of the devil."

Paul, full of the Holy Ghost, under the anointing, addressed Elymas, the sorcerer, as "you seed, you son of the devil, you enemy of all righteousness."

Any seed of the devil is an enemy of righteousness.

SIN AND CONSEQUENCE

> *...will you not cease perverting the straight ways of the Lord? And now, indeed, the hand of the Lord is upon you, and you shall be blind, not seeing the sun for a time.*
> (Acts 13:10-11)

Remember, God does not fight fair. He made it clear that the Seed of the woman will bruise the head of the serpent. That power and authority to bruise was given to Paul because he was carrying the Seed of the woman, which is the Word of God. Paul, being full of the Holy Ghost, looked at the seed of the serpent and made a decree

67

that because of what he was doing, he would be blind from that day forward.

"For turning people away from the faith and from righteousness, you shall be blind from this day forward."

The Bible says immediately, not the next day, not the next year, immediately a mist came upon his face and he could not see - he had to look for somebody to lead him.

BLINDED BY THE LIGHT

Many may say we are living in a generation where God does not act in that way anymore, but let me tell you, even if He does not do those same things in the physical, He does indeed do things like that in the spirit.

If you turn away from righteousness, you will become blinded in the spirit, and not know your way forward. You will begin going around in circles; nothing will work for you any more, because you allowed the serpent to put his seed in you.

When you contest with the Seed of the woman that has been ordained to bruise your head, when that Seed opens His mouth and makes a pronouncement, you can be the king of the land, but it shall still come pass.

CHAPTER EIGHT

In the Fullness of Time

Isaiah foretold the coming of the Seed of the woman:

Therefore the Lord Himself will give you a sign: Behold, the virgin shall conceive and bear a Son, and shall call His name Immanuel.

(Isaiah 7:14)

This passage is picked up again in Luke, Chapter One:

And behold, you will conceive in your womb and bring forth a Son, and shall call His name Jesus. He will be great, and will be called the Son of the Highest; and the Lord God will give Him the throne of His father David. And He will reign over the house of Jacob forever, and of His kingdom there will be no end.
Then Mary said to the angel, "How can this be, since I do not know a man?"
And the angel answered and said to her, "The Holy Spirit will come upon you, and the power of the Highest will overshadow you; therefore, also, that Holy One who is to be born will be called the Son of God.

(Luke 1:31-35)

All of this took place exactly when God intended:

> *But when the fullness of the time had come, God sent forth His Son, born of a woman, born under the law to redeem those who were under the law, that we might receive the adoption as sons.*
>
> (Galatians 4:4-5)

NOURISHING THE SEED

But God's work was not yet complete. More preparation was in order:

> *Then Jesus came from Galilee to John at the Jordan to be baptized by him. And John tried to prevent Him, saying, 'I need to be baptized by You, and are You coming to me?'*
> *But Jesus answered and said to him, 'Permit it to be so now...'*
>
> (Matthew 3:13-15)

Similarly, there are some things that you need to permit to be so, for now, in order to nourish the seed within you. "I know that I am going to be greater than you, but I am going to permit it to be so for now; I am going to humble myself."

SO THE SCRIPTURE MAY BE FULFILLED

> *In the beginning was the Word, and the Word was with God, and the Word was God.*
>
> (John 1:1)

And the Word became flesh and dwelt among us,
and we beheld His glory, the glory as of the only
begotten of the Father, full of grace and truth.
(John 1:14)

Mary conceived the Word, and in the fullness of time God sent His Son, born of the woman according to the law, and the Word become flesh and dwelt among men. Then the Word went to John the Baptist and told him, "I want you to immerse me, I want you to baptize Me, that all Scripture will be fulfilled."

John the Baptist took the Word, which was the Seed of the woman, and baptized the Word. When he baptized the Word, the Word came up from the water praying, the heavens were opened and the Spirit of the Lord came down in the bodily form of a dove and sat upon the Word.

The letter killeth, but the Spirit giveth life. It does not matter how much Scripture you read; if the Spirit of the Lord does not descend upon the Word so that it may be quickened, then the Word is of no effect.

HIS SEAL OF APPROVAL

The Spirit of the Lord descended and sat upon the Word, and the Word was quickened. Then the Father spoke from Heaven, saying, *"This is My beloved Son"*... and the Word became the Son. In other words, the Word became flesh and dwelt among men. The Seed of the woman prophesied in Genesis 3:15 had now manifested, and God had placed His seal of approval upon it; He had endorsed the Word.

71

Many seeds had come, but none of them heard God's voice. Since this was the Seed that was spoken of in Genesis 3:15, the voice of the Father was heard and He said, *"This is My beloved Son in whom I am well pleased."*

Sojourn in the Wilderness

When the Word came up from the water, the Word was driven by the Spirit into the wilderness to be tried and tested. God released the Word to go to the wilderness to contend with the devil. The Word went into the wilderness, not driven by a devil, not driven by a demon; the Bible says the Spirit of the Sovereign Lord drove the Word, led the Word, compelled the Word to go into the wilderness so that they could have an open confrontation.

The Word was in the desert and for forty days and forty nights, fasting, eating nothing. After the forty days were over, the devil, the tempter, came to the Word and he began to test and to try and to tempt the Word.

When you have conceived the Seed and you have brought forth the Seed, the day will come, the season will come when the Seed will be driven to the wilderness to be tested and to be tried by the devil.

When the devil appeared to Jesus, he knew that His body was weak from fasting, so the first temptation was to turn stones into bread. "Come on, Jesus, I know You are hungry, I know what Your flesh needs, all you have to do is make room to accommodate it."

WILL YOU PASS THE TEST?

You have just given birth to the Word, to the Seed that will bruise the head of the serpent, and you receive a prophecy. What are you going to do with what you have received?

You are born again, filled with the Holy Ghost, speaking in the tongues of men and the tongues of angels; you have been endorsed as a son of God in whom He is well pleased, because you are in your place of purpose. Now you must go to the wilderness and fight.

Drugs, alcohol, sexual perversion - the same thing that you have been delivered from is the same test you will face after you have birthed the seed. The devil will come and contend and contest that seed that is going to bruise his head. Therefore, it is vitally important that you know the Word of God.

SPEAK THE WORD

At each temptation, Jesus was able to fire back at the devil and say, "Devil, I see you, I feel you, I smell you, but it is written that man shall not live by bread alone, but by every Word that proceeds out of the mouth of God!"

So Jesus overcame the devil.

Notice, the devil obviously finds time to read the Word. The devil knows the Word; he just does not apply it and receive it. The devil knows the Word although he does not apply it correctly, but many children of God, the only time they open their Bibles is when they come to church on Sunday! Take the time to read the Word.

The devil did not quote anything but the Word. He went to Deuteronomy 8, then he went on to Psalm 91 and he said, "It is written that if You fall and jump, God has given His angels charge over You and will not let Your foot dash upon a stone."

When the devil comes to you and I as children of God, he comes with a half word, but because we do not know the full Word, because the Word is not dwelling in us in all wisdom, we do not know how to counter the devil with the Word!

Jesus countered the devil with the Word.

The Devil Is Not Impressed

The devil is not impressed with you; you can jump, skip, hula and roll, and even froth at the mouth, carry on all you want...the devil is not impressed.

The men and women who intimidate the devil are those who have the Seed in their bellies, who have the Word. The devil has to think twice before he comes to them.

Give God a Reference

You can cry all night, "Oh! My husband left me; he took off with Sally down the street..." but God is not even listening.

Instead, He is saying, "Give me a reference. I watch over My Word, not your words. I am so committed to fulfilling My Word that when you give me a reference out of my Word it cannot return empty, it must accomplish a purpose."

"Well God, You know I love You, You know I do this and that..."

But God says, "What does my Word say?"

You cannot come against a person that is full of the Word; he will beat you every time. You can speak in tongues all you want, but as long as that person is armed with the Word, don't go there, because the Word is like arrows being shot out of the quiver. Every arrow that hits the devil lessens his effect.

Jesus overcame the devil with the Word. He said, *"It is written."*

YOUR OWN PERSONAL WILDERNESS

You must win the battle in your personal wilderness before God puts you on display for the real battle. Champions are not trained in the ring. Champions are trained in the desert. When you make your appearance in that ring, that is not the time for you to rehearse. First you go out and work that treadmill, sweating away. Once the bell rings, the fight is on, and it will be obvious how much training you had in the desert.

The devil laughs at Christians because we use what the Bible calls "vain repetition."

And when you pray, do not use vain repetitions as the heathen do. For they think that they will be heard for their many words.

(Matthew 6:7)

The devil says, "Ha! Those words have no power."

But let a man come against the devil after he has been in the wilderness – and he will be a threat.

Once you have won the battle of the flesh, the spirit rises.

RETURN IN POWER

The Bible says, "He went, filled with the Holy Ghost, but He returned in the power of the Spirit."

When Jesus overcame the devil in the wilderness, He returned in the power, the "dunamis," the power that demonstrates the power of God.

The Word in you, the Seed in you, can never stand out until you have won the wrestling match in the wilderness. That is when you curse a tumor and it dries up. That is when you command the dead to be resurrected and they are!

Once you win the match, you return in power.

The Bible says when the Word returned, He returned in the power.

CHAPTER NINE

For This Purpose

He who sins is of the devil, for the devil has sinned from the beginning. For this purpose the Son of God was manifested, that He might destroy the works of the devil.

(1 John 3:8)

TO DESTROY THE WORKS OF THE DEVIL

"For this purpose." Jesus, the Seed of the woman, was manifested and revealed for one purpose, that He might "luo," destroy, undo the works of the devil. For the three years that Jesus was manifested, for the three years that He walked upon the face of the earth, He walked with purpose, He talked with purpose, He ate with purpose, He slept with purpose. His eye was focused; He was not double-minded. He was not confused concerning His assignment; He knew that God had sent Him on earth for one thing and one thing only, to bruise the head of the serpent, and to destroy his works.

WHAT ARE THE WORKS OF THE ENEMY?

Now the works of the flesh are evident, which are: adultery, fornication, uncleanness, lewdness, idolatry, sorcery, hatred, contentions, jealousies, outbursts of wrath, selfish ambitions, dissensions, heresies, envy, murders, drunkenness, revelries, and the like; of which I tell you beforehand, just as I also told you in time past, that those who practice such things will not inherit the Kingdom of God (Galatians 5:19-21).

We must also understand our purpose; we must know the enemy's works that we are to destroy.

CRUSH HIS HEAD!

"And the God of peace will crush Satan under your feet shortly" (Romans 16:20).

The Seed of the woman which is the Word of God is in your belly, and God has given you power to crush the head of the serpent.

Think about every seed of the devil that has hindered your progress, hindered your destiny, hindered your purpose. God says,

> *I have given you power and authority* '*...to trample on serpents and scorpions, and over all the power of the enemy, and nothing shall by any means hurt you.'*
>
> (Luke 10:19)

It Is Time for War

I want you to know that your feet are anointed. Right now, begin to trample with all of your might every power, every spirit, every wicked and evil damnable entity that has hindered you, your family, your progress, your finances, and begin to crush the head of the serpent in the name of Jesus! Crush poverty, crush sickness, crush disease, crush unforgiveness. It is time for war! Crush the devil, crush cancer, crush HIV, crush leukemia, crush the works of the devil, crush witchcraft, crush sorcery, crush divination!

God has empowered you, God has anointed you, God has released you: "the Seed of the woman shall crush the head of the serpent." God has given you authority to trample upon scorpions and serpents and all the works of the enemy and nothing whatsoever shall harm you, so crush poverty, crush lack, crush inefficiency, crush the devil who is coming against your marriage!

Thank God for the victory!

CHAPTER TEN

The Mystery Has Been Revealed

So we understand God declared war between the kingdom of Satan and His Kingdom, and as a result, since Creation, there has been enmity between man and the devil. In addition, it is clear that this enmity has caused, and will continue to cause, strife throughout history.

Genesis 3:15 contains a revelation that will forever change your life!

And I will put enmity between you and the woman, and between your seed and her seed. He shall bruise your head, and you shall bruise His heel.

Who is the seed?

Galatians 3:16 says,

Now to Abraham and his seed were the promises made. He saith not, And to seeds, as of many; but as of one, and to thy Seed, which is Christ.

Therefore, the Seed is Christ.

However, in Colossians 1:26-27,

> *...a great mystery which has been hid from ages and from generations, but now is made manifest to his saints to whom God would make known what is the riches of the glory of this mystery among the Gentiles; which is Christ IN YOU, the Hope of Glory.*

Therefore, **Christ, the Word of God** that became flesh is now IN YOU. You child of God are carrying that seed! It is your destiny to bruise the head of the enemy. Whatever demonic devices that are trying to kill you and your purpose, all you have to do is put them under your feet, apply the Word of God, which is the Seed that was promised to bruise the head of the serpent whether it's cancer, poverty, depression or addictions – use the Seed, IN YOU to bruise the head of the enemy and walk in victory.

Christ, the Word of God who became flesh is now IN YOU – use the seed, IN YOU to bruise the head of the enemy and walk in victory.

Child of God – you are *Licensed to Bruise*!

The purpose of this book has been to reveal the secret behind this mysterious passage. We have studied in depth the meaning of the Seed and the power it carries. And most meaningfully, we have discovered that we are already carrying that power; we are filled with that Seed. The tragedy is that many of this generation are unaware, and their Seed lies dormant within them.

ACTIVATING THE SEED WITHIN US

In order to wage effective warfare against the enemy, therefore, we understand that the Seed must not remain dormant; we need to activate that Seed. We learned that every time we pray, read the Word, attend church, we are activating the Seed. In addition, we understand that it is the revelation of the Word that motivates and enables us to fight. It does not matter how much Scripture we read; if the Spirit of the Lord does not descend upon the Word so that it may be quickened, then the Word is of no effect.

Once we receive the revelation of God's Word, we are able to build and to stand firmly against the onslaught of the enemy. Through revelation, the Seed will be quickened and God will take us into new dimensions in Him.

WAGING GOOD WARFARE

The Seed inside of us has been specifically designed, like a mercenary, to bruise the head of the serpent. When God's prophetic word has been released into our spirit, it must accomplish that purpose for which it was designed. God says, "I am so committed to fulfilling My Word that it cannot return empty, it must accomplish its purpose."

Unfortunately, the devil is diligently watching over that prophetic word, and will do everything possible to quench it. He knows that if he can deceive us or get us out from under the protection of God's covering, he is able to battle us more effectively. Therefore it is imperative that we understand the responsibility that accompanies carrying the seed.

TAKING CARE OF THE VESSEL

First, we discovered that if our vessels, our bodies, are defiled, we cannot carry the anointing. Sin must have no place in us. If we choose sin, if we choose to walk under a curse, we realize that we are acting as the seed of the enemy, and that the consequences will eventually influence not only us, but our third, fourth, even fifth generations.

- We must not fall to the spirit of pride; instead we must be filled with obedience and humility.

- We must be careful that we do not sow seeds of discord, that we are not instigators.

- We understand that every time we stumble, it is because we have allowed the serpent to bite our heels with unforgiveness, anger or animosity.

- We must set aside a time and place of communion with God, where we meet Him on a consistent basis. But we know that our fasting and prayer cannot manipulate God. God works in the fullness of time; He will not move just because He wants to make us happy.

TRAINING IN THE WILDERNESS

When we have finally brought forth the Seed, the day will come when we will be driven to the wilderness to be tested by the devil, just as Jesus was. And whatever it was that we were delivered from will be the same test we face in the desert.

Champions are formed through practice; therefore we must win this battle in the wilderness before God can employ us in the war.

The Seed in us can never stand in battle until we have won the wrestling match in the wilderness.

USING THE SEED

We are aware that someone, somewhere, is waiting for the power that is within us. The Seed we are carrying contains a salvation, a miracle, for someone God will set in our path. We must be diligent to use the seed at the proper time.

One of the dynamics of battle is that we may be wounded as the seed within us fights the enemy's seed. Knowing this, when we are bruised, we simply get up, brush ourselves off, and continue on. We know that when we fight for the Lord, no weapon formed against us will prosper.

We understand that the victory is ultimately ours.

In every generation, there are those who have carried the seed, those of faith who have believed God and fought for Him. They fight the seeds of the enemy: poverty, sickness, infirmity, lack, insufficiency. God has divinely permitted these men and women to bruise the head of the serpent, while the serpent may only strike the heel of the Seed of the woman. And no one has ever died of a bruised heel.

When we strike the head of the serpent, we make his efforts fruitless. Without the head, the rest of the body is aimless and ineffective.

For the three years that Jesus ministered, He walked with purpose, He talked with purpose, because He understood His destiny.

Jesus understood His destiny.

Likewise, so must we.

FINALLY

If you've never accepted Jesus Christ as your Savior – please take a moment to say this prayer:

Lord Jesus, forgive me for all my sins, I repent from my ways. Wash me in Your blood and cleanse me from all unrighteousness. I believe that You died on the cross, were buries, and on the third day God the Father raised You from the dead. Right now, Lord Jesus, I open the door to my heard and I receive You into my heart as my Lord and personal Savior. Amen.

If you prayed that prayer, you qualify to be a partaker of the Seed, and to bruise the head of the enemy.

God bless you!

TEACHING TAPE, CD, AND DVD SERIES

By Rev. Sarah Morgan

Seed of the Woman; Genesis 3:15   **3 Tapes: $15**

Genesis 3:15 contains a revelation that will forever change your life!

> *And l will put enmity between you and the woman, and between your seed and her seed. He shall bruise your head and you shall bruise his heel.*

You are carrying that seed! It is your destiny to bruise the head of the enemy. Whatever demonic devices are trying to kill you and your purpose, all you have to do is put them under your feet, apply the Word of God, which is the Seed that was promised to bruise the head of the serpent, whether you are battling cancer, poverty, depression or addictions.

Galatians 3:16 says,

> *Now to Abraham and his seed were the promises made. He saith not, And to seeds, as of many; but as of one, and to thy Seed, which is Christ.*

Therefore, the Seed is Christ. However, in Colossians 1:26, 27

> *...a great mystery which has been hid from ages and from generations, but now is made manifest to his saints to whom God would make known what is the riches of the glory of this mystery among the Gentiles; which is Christ IN YOU, the Hope of Glory.*

Therefore, Christ, the Word of God who became flesh is now IN YOU — use the seed, IN YOU to bruise the head of the enemy and walk in victory.

Child of God — you are *Licensed to Bruise*!

When Zion Travailed, She Birthed! 2 DVD's: $20

In this dynamic 2 DVD series the Holy Spirit will minister to you. As you begin to understand what is growing on the inside of you, you can change a generation! You'll be pregnant with destiny once you accept this revelation; the Spirit of the Lord will act as a midwife and encourage you to push your baby out! In spite of every contraction, know that your pain has a purpose. Your Life will never be the same after you experience this series.

Woman on a Mission!; Matthew 26:6-13 2 CD's: $15

Your mission, should you choose to accept, is Jesus. Go into the world and preach the gospel; become an effective witness. You are to leave an indelible mark on family, community, and the nations.

Ouch! Jesus Fix Me; Numbers 12   4 CD's: $25

Miriam had to deal with jealousy; David had to deal with lust; what are you dealing with? If you do not confront your sin, you will conform to your sin! Good medicine is bitter. Yell Ouch! And let Jesus fix you!

The Travailer Has a Mark; Isaiah 66:8   3 CD's: $20

When you travail you will prevail! The purpose of your travail is to create an opening in order to bring forth a measure of life or growth. If the opening of the natural womb is enlarged to bring forth the baby, so it is in the realm of the spirit. When you begin to travail through prayer and fasting, crying out to God, your spiritual womb begins to be enlarged. The vision, purpose, dream that you're carrying, the baby that you are carrying, in other words the Word of God that is in your belly, is getting ready to come forth.

Sing O' Barren; Isaiah 54:1-3   3 CD's: $20

Sing is God-focused; you are commanded to do this. Barren is man-focused; your focus is constantly on your lack. Our wombs are closed because we never open our mouths to praise and sing. Your solution, remedy or power comes when you open your mouth and sing because He uses the foolish things to confound the wicked. Somewhere between the sigh and the song is sight. The song is what confronts the barrenness. The answer for your problem is "Sing...", for the song of the Lord will expand your kingdom.

For more ministry products please visit our website at: www.womenofvisionla.org

TEACHING TAPE, CD, AND DVD SERIES

By Bishop Peter Morgan

Calling All Things into Divine Alignment: 7 Nights of Seeking God — 15 Tapes: $75

This series includes three Powerful sermons preached over a 7-Night Revival; You Can Be Free from Bondage: until you become disgusted at where you are, you can't launch out to where you are supposed to be. You need to be set free. Better Things: any time you dwell on the past you lose space in your mind for the future. God has a set mark for you to attain, you no longer have to settle for mediocrity. Waging War According to the Prophetic: the prophetic word in your life must be taken seriously. If treated carelessly, our lives will lose its direction (a bonus message by Rev. Sarah Morgan).

God's Intention to Prosper You — 3 Tapes: $15

The secret of success and prosperity is obedience. Learn the four great benefits of obedience. Everything that God has created was created by principles. Your blessings are not determined by location but by God, according to you living by His principles.

Maturity: A Mark of Christian Success   11 CD's: $80

Grow up, get in line! Children fight but adults solve problems. Is your church full of babies? The greatest enemy of man is ignorance. Because we have cheapened Christianity, we've gotten cheap results. The ten characteristics of a mature Christian are explained in this dynamic and comprehensive teaching series. Includes the sermon "Faith on Fire": How well you understand the scriptures will determine how far in life you go. When you have "Faith on Fire" you aren't bound by barriers, you don't fear principalities. Moving on in spite of is Faith on Fire!

The Noble Christian   2 Tapes: $10

A "must have" series for dealing with integrity, reliability and commitment.

The Right Time   3 CD's: $20

You can have skill, talent, knowledge or potential, but if you do not value time and you use it wrong, you will not get your desired results. Knowledge has to combine with the proper investment of time for fruit to be born out of it. In this teaching series you will learn of God's Divine itinerary and principles on how to make the most of the time given you.

For more ministry products please visit our website at: www.visionintlm.com

FREE SHIPPING ON ORDERS OVER $45

Qty	Item Name	Price	Total
		SUBTOTAL	
		TAX DEDUCTABLE LOVE GIFT	
	10% SHIPPING ON ORDERS $45 OR UNDER		
		TOTAL AMOUNT ENCLOSED	

ORDER FORM

Name_____

Address _____

City_____ St_____ Zip _____

Pastor Sarah Morgan
Contact Info

Mailing Address:
PO Box 361074
Los Angeles, Ca 90036

www.visionintlm.com
www.womenofvisionla.org

Email: visionintlm@aol.com
Phone: 888-846-4VIM (4846)

Contact

Please contact us with any questions you may have and we will respond as soon as we can. Our ministry staff will address your feedback, requests or questions.

Booking Information

Are you interested in having Pastor Sarah Morgan speak at your upcoming conference, meeting or worship service? We would love to hear from you. For booking information please visit our website at:

www.womenofvisionala.org

Or contact my administrator, Shirley Brown at:

323-309-2259 or 888-846-4VIM